Richard F

Smart Boy Wanted

Illustrations by James and Liam Raftery

Cover photograph by Elizabeth Hope

Smithy Publications

Copyright © 2003 Richard Raftery

The right of Richard Raftery to be identified as the author of the work has been asserted by him in accordance with the Copyright, Designs and Patents Act 1988

All rights reserved. No part of this publication may be reproduced, stored in a retrieval system, or transmitted, in any form or means without the prior written permission of the publisher, nor be otherwise circulated in any form of binding or cover other than that in which it is published and without a similar condition being imposed on the subsequent purchaser.

Published in Great Britain
by
Smithy Publications
PO Box 32
Leeds
LS8 2BS

Printed and bound in Great Britain by Resource Print Solutions (Leeds)

ISBN 0-9545935-0-2

Acknowledgements

Thanks are due to everyone who has given me support and encouragement over the last few years giving me the impetus to 'get out there and do it'.

I would especially like to thank, in no particular order; 'Our Kev' and Jackie, Sue and Tony Ashdown, Mike and Mary Garner, Lucia and Derek Glenn, Christine and Paul Hamill, Jo and Jo's mum, Seamus and Belinda Markey, Linda Coffey, Liz Trifunovic, Dave and Kath Johns, Graeme and Kathleen Johnstone, Ron and Pat Hartley, Gerry Beaumont, Pete and Viv Brownrigg, Johnny and Jackie Doyle, Mickie and Sue Teggart, 'Bjorg', Pauline and Ted Woolley, Michael Deenican R.I.P., and everyone else down at the 'Maccy'. Catherine Shelton (*the flame-haired playwright*), Riggsy, Simon Guilfoyle, Ruth Hancock, Deryn Porter, Lyndsey and Kerry Hazlewood, Angela Neville, Austin Danks R.I.P. and all the other '*Wortleyites*'; Dave Mayers, Andy Tidswell and all the *Old Intakonians*, Colin Noble, Brendan Ego, Kathryn Seymour (*DJ extraordinaire*), Ray Middleton (*Web Genius*), and most importantly my wife Christine, who has had a lot to endure since I started compiling this collection.

For
Christine, Jane, James and Liam

Contents

	page
Raftery the Poet	1
Billy the Backward Boy	2
The Wasp	4
Life, Death and Football	5
The Dead Shepherd	7
Two Bean Cans on a String	9
Maundy Thursday '68	11
Potato Picking	13
The Maoist Demo	15
The Black Magician	16
The Beer Bottle Baron of Bootle	18
The Keck King	21
The Day Out (minus the Croaker) 1969	23
Sick Will	24
Morgo's Programmes	26
The Milk Thief	28
Thorax	29
Ormskirk New Year 1971	31
The Plate Spinner	33
Midnight Ghosts	36
The Lakes	38
Lunch Break-up	39
Dyslexia	41
The Walton Wedding	42
The Shadow Boxer	45
The Last Taxi Ride	46
Gobbed in Town	47
Mental in the Fens	50
The Timelord	53
The Middling, Muddling Years	54
Wilfred Benitez	56
No Ribbons Needed	58
Vanessa's Thong	59
The Tattooed Lady's Son	60
Mad Lap Dancing Woman (The Curse of Ceaucescu)	61

Dad	64
Sharon and Karen, Shane and Wayne (a.k.a. The Kids from Fame)	66
The Incredible Suntanned Woman	68
Smart Boy Wanted	69
Holiday in Yarmouth	71
The Tight Get	73
Raftery's Flip-flop Solution	76
Soldiering Boy	78
It came in the Night	80

Raftery the Poet

My name is Raftery the poet
My epitaph may well one day read
Quite good in a so-so sort of way
But not all he cracked himself up to be

Billy (the backward boy)

Poor Billy Matthews was in our class
Aged ten and still in the bottom set
He sat with those who were half his age
In my mind I see him yet
Day after day, year after year
Wondering when his time was up
Same books, same sums, while faces change
They came and went, but he stayed put
Each day as always, the grind, the pain
Torment and humiliation
Each morning back he'd come again
To endure more degradation

'Can mat cat sat
Sat can dad sad'
Day in, day out
I would go mad
'Man hat lad had
Rat fan ran fad'
Year in, year out
So sad, too bad

I can still picture the painful scene
Hard at work the morning long
Fingers clutching, pencil scratching
Easy sums, but all done wrong
Mrs Gibson ranting, shouting
'Think harder boy! Use your loaf!'
Flinging book across the classroom
'Useless idiot, shambling oaf!'
Wooden ruler, hand outstretched
Mouth wide open, on tiptoe
Sharp cracks echo around the room
He paid the price for being slow

'One two is two
Two twos are four'
Outside, blue sky
Nearby, the open door
'Three twos are six
Four twos are nine'
'Wrong again specimen
Stay in at playtime'

Deep down, what did he really feel?
When called upon to stand and suffer
The pain of the strap across his wrist
Which only seemed to make him tougher
Although the tears fell quick enough
Yet, he seemed to endure it all
With a strange kind of stoicism
Supported by some inner wall
As if deep down he understood
That his tormentor and his jailor
Had no real power or solution
She was, perhaps, the failure

'Old Lob.... is the.... master
Mr Dan .....is Old Lob's..... dog'
'Read it faster, read it faster
Slowcoach boy, get it read!
Idiot boy, well turned ten
Start again, start again!'
'Old Lob's cat ... is Miss Tibbs'
(Wish Old Lob would go to hell)

The Wasp

Aged seven and listening to Mrs Gibson,
giving out about the flood
With Noah and his Ark and his raven
and the eternal struggle between evil and good
I reached my hand furtively to my collar,
hoping she would not see
So that I might deal with whatever it was
which conspired to irritate me
A wasp stung my finger! I gritted my teeth
and thrust my hand under the desk
Daring not to speak out or make any expression,
(her reaction you never could guess)
I clutched my finger for the whole afternoon
Home-time took forever to come
At half three I ran home in tears
and told the sad tale to my mum
Who at once produced a pungent ointment,
which took away some of the ache
But the thought of the boy afraid to cry out
continued to keep me awake
The following week, at the end of the morning,
we said, as usual, the prayers
Plus one Hail Mary, for Mrs Yeats - dinner lady,
who'd been stung by a wasp in her hair
It doesn't do to suffer in silence
You'll get sold short in the end
No prayers or special intentions,
Just pain and more pain, without end

Life, Death and Football

There were some kids who travelled by taxi,
(it looked like a bit of a laugh).
Journeying in from no bus land,
way out in Bickerstaffe.
An ancient, trundling, black vehicle.
An aging, frail man at the wheel.
Spluttering along down country lanes,
past hedge and ditch and field.
Never likely to break the speed limit
and in winter, when weather got worse,
if even a slight mist descended,
he'd slow to the speed of a hearse.

At school, one Friday, we were kicking around.
It was January and a biting wind blew.
Suddenly we saw the taxi kids,
but the cab was nowhere in view.
'Michael fell out!' they yelled to everyone,
as they ran inside the gate.
'He banged his head upon the kerb,
that's why we're running late.'
'There was a pool of blood upon the road,
they've taken him away.'
'We don't know if he'll live or die,
the ambulance wouldn't say.'

A hushed silence quickly descended,
spreading across the playground.
The icy wind blew even louder,
as if death was in that sound.
People stood in huddled groups,
not knowing what to do.
Aware that these things happen,
but not to those we knew.

'Oh well,' said my brother, breaking the spell,
'We might as well finish the game,'
And Susan Harvey looked straight at him,
speaking angrily and unrestrained.
'That little boy might be dead,' she cried,
'You heard what they said about the blood.'
'Yes,' said my brother, 'but I don't really think
standing around is going to do any good.'

He did have a point, I will admit,
yet nobody took up his call.
Some looked up the street for a hopeful sign,
others stood and stared at the wall.
The headmistress brought us in as usual
and then we assembled and prayed,
for Maggie's mum still in hospital
and also that Michael be saved.
By mid morning things were much calmer,
when we heard the latest news.
He wasn't too badly injured at all,
just shaken and bandaged and bruised
On mid winter mornings, I think of this moment,
when it's ice-cold, and you can see your breath.
That for some people, including my brother,
football takes precedence over life and death.

The Dead Shepherd

Where is Joey Kyrylenko's dad?
Is it true he just went mad?
By the fire last Saturday night
Eyes blood red and face turned white
Swept things off the mantelpiece
Said the pain would never cease
Smashed the teapot and the clock
Left them all in a state of shock
Couldn't take it any more
Grabbed his coat and slammed the door
The mother weeping with the lad
Where is Joey Kyrylenko's dad?

Where is Joey Kyrylenko's dad?
Why does Joey look so sad?
Why is he staring at his shoes?
Has he heard some recent news?
Two weeks have gone since dad was here
What made him want to disappear?
To just take off and run away
Leaving those behind to pray
Vanishing without a trace
An empty seat by a fireplace
Can things have really been that bad?
Where is Joey Kyrylenko's dad?

Life could never be the same
When he fled from the Ukraine
Been in a camp for quite some time
Images printed on his mind
A mis-spelt name upon a list
A number tattooed on a wrist

When death is closer than any friend
Then you long for it all to end
A new world beckoned but even so
It's very hard to just let go
Memories can drive you mad
Where is Joey Kyrylenko's dad?

They found his dad after a while
Over the hill, beyond the style
Where blackbirds sang and skylarks flew
Across the field where barley grew
Down the path all deep in mud
Way out yonder in Butcher's wood
Three weeks after he first took flight
Watching sheep by pale moonlight
Eyes wide open – there to see
Swinging from his gallows tree
Relatives wept their bitter tears
But he'd been dead for many years

Two Bean Cans on a String

You bought some beer from the offy
like a real street corner kid
But when you thought no one was looking
you poured it down the grid
You said that with your air pistol
you shot your neighbour's cat
But who threw up in the science lab
when we cut up that dead rat?
You said you had the complete set
of Mars Attacks, no doubt
But when we went to see them
your mum had thrown them out
You said your walkie-talkie
was the very latest thing
But in your garden shed we saw
two bean cans on a string

Monstrous boy, monstrous boy
Obnoxious twerp, repellent youth
With your singular inability
to ever tell the truth

You bragged about your holiday
with your mum and dad in Wales
You said it was a posh hotel
with gilded beams and rails
But of course we all knew better
it was just a load of tripe
And strange it was that the girls you met
were never quite your type

Your ten-speed rally racer
was the butcher boys cast off
Your black belt in Kung fu
was just a piece of stolen cloth
Your wonderful amplifier
of which we heard so much

A transistor radio stuffed inside
a converted rabbit hutch

Monstrous boy, monstrous boy
Obnoxious twerp, repellent youth
With your singular inability
to ever tell the truth

You walked into the youthy one
night
and joined the hard card school
Lost all your money playing poker
then sat there like a fool
With a borrowed trilby on your head
cocked on to one side
Said you only did it for a laugh
but once again you lied

Monstrous boy, monstrous boy
Obnoxious twerp, repellent youth
With your singular inability
to ever tell the truth

offy - Off License.
Mars Attacks – in the sixties these were a series of bubblegum cards depicting an attack by Martians.
Youthy – youth club.

Maundy Thursday '68

Away to mass at gone seven thirty,
altar serving with John O' Hare
Walking down beside the beech trees,
polished shoes and flattened hair
'Those Paper Dolls,' he gushed in haste,
'Weren't they fabulous? Weren't they great?'
(Top of the Pops had kept us indoors,
out of breath and running late)
Struggling with the rusty fastening,
on the old wrought iron gate
Tested and found somewhat lacking,
on Maundy Thursday, sixty eight

I heard but made no sharp riposte,
as we hurried through the sacristy door
The musty smell of snuffed out candles,
while truth lay dying on the floor
The Paper Dolls - a vocal trio,
anachronistic even then
Blonde wigs and matching satin dresses,
Barbie dolls for older men
The song they sang, such shallow drivel,
'Something here (here, here) in my heart'
No fan was I, nor never would be,
O'Hare and I were miles apart

The Canon entered with a flourish,
'Come on lads, its time to start'
Altar wine, unleavened bread,
but something twisted in my heart
Glancing through the lead lined windows,
skeletal ruins of Gerard Hall
Hidden altars and furtive masses,
secret tunnels behind the wall
The tortured martyrs' faith surviving,
their fire, sword and dungeon fate
Yet I would lie by staying silent,
on Maundy Thursday, sixty eight

Beyond the sunset a new dawn flickered,
a generation seeking change
With velvet cloak the ice was melting,
and suddenly the world was strange
Old certainties began to crumble,
 it was forbidden to forbid
Seeking sand beneath the cobbles,
modern martyrs stood and bled
Despite the backlash, (tanks soon rolling),
the game was up, the hour was late
No show of strength could turn the clocks back,
by Maundy Thursday, sixty eight

Potato picking

All the shrinking days one October half term
Back when I was fourteen
We picked potatoes, me and the brother
Out in a West Lancashire field
Loading up bags at considerable speed
Backs bent for most of the day
Scooping up thousands of fresh grown potatoes
And slinging the bad ones away
Lads out from Kirkby, effing and blinding
Grafting like never before
A few with posh voices ventured from Aughton
All well worn out by half four
A transistor radio gave out tinny pop music
Lulu was high in the charts
The tractor broke down and we all sat around
While they raced off to find a spare part
The brother made his own sandwiches
White bread laced with tomato ketch
He downed them all quickly and then disappeared
Soon after we all heard him retch
It stayed quite dry for most of the week
The sky was clear each day
Each afternoon's end we trailed back with our friends
Intent on collecting our pay
Then riding off homewards on our rusty bikes
Like the Boys of the Old Brigade
We had only one lamp between us
As we saw the autumn light fade
At home with our tea inside us
Bikes now parked in the shed
Consumed by incredible exhaustion
We went unusually early to bed
We must have made some real money
Working long hours each day

But the demands on our pockets were many
And it soon got frittered away
Whatever it might have been spent on
Must surely have brought me some joy
But the memories have longer stayed with me
Of spud picking when I was a boy

The Maoist Demo

A house match final was being played and we were told to watch
as the rain fell gently over the mud stained playing field.
But a few of us were not over enthused or interested very much,
we huddled up together like a humid, human shield.
Then Big Monna had a great idea and said 'Now listen lads,
it's time to advance the cause of communism in one nation.'
So on that wet, Wednesday afternoon the progressive youth of Bootle
went all ultra radical and staged a Maoist demonstration

There was Big Monna, the Croaker and me and Gozzy Nolan,
charging up and down the touchline, chanting 'Mao tse Tung'.
Waving our little red books got from lads whose dads were dockers.
Soon to be joined by all manner of patheticos and hangers on.
Big Monna said 'American imperialism is like a paper tiger'
and I said 'Political power grows out of the barrel of a gun'.
'The peasants,' said Croaker, 'are the sea in which the guerrilla swims'
and Pob said we were being offensive and he would get us done.

We were organized and ready like a well-oiled fighting machine.
With the peasantry we were poised to forge a strong alliance.
This was a red revolution spreading like a flower,
a massive and subversive gesture of defiance.
We were primed and willing to fight and die standing,
our wisdom we exclaimed with mighty roars.
Shaking off the binding chains of capitalist oppression,
blood shedding martyrs for the struggle and the cause

All too soon we were apprehended and sternly brought to justice.
Seemingly the powers that be were visibly shaken.
We were given a severe warning and an after school detention,
our punishment for staging the Maoist demonstration.
Big Monna said 'It goes to show how proletarian power
will overthrow the ruling classes and bring them to their knees,
The sword of revolution is forged on the anvil of struggle.'
We said 'He's right you know!' and ran off home to have our teas.

The Black Magician

At school some were well into footy,
or making planes from airfix kits
But one stood apart from all of this,
denouncing us all as twits
With tortoiseshell NHS glasses
and hair like red Weetabix
He re-invented himself as the Black Magician,
demonstrating diabolical tricks
Consulting obscure weighty tomes,
as well as arcane law
Into prophecy and necromancy,
a medieval bore
He was always ready to cast a spell
with a useful, appropriate quote
Advising on black magic etiquette,
the correct way to slaughter a goat
If you mentioned any ailments,
he'd offer you a potion
And tell you to rub in at midnight,
some loathsome, unpleasant lotion

I went to school with the Black Magician
but he didn't start out that way
With sellotaped specs and wayfinder shoes,
like 'Just William' on an off day
So we did not get over excited,
we took it all in our stride
He was after all just a schoolboy
and sometimes we could be quite snide
He'd blether about evil spirits
inside the science lab
Some thought it quite hilarious,
a genuine load of gab
In his garden shed he'd keep
an assorted strange collection
Books on Beelzebub and Ouija Boards,
hidden to avoid detection
Jars of foul smelling substances
and dead things tied up with string
Tins of rotting, flaking insects
were a few of his favourite things

I went to school with the Black Magician
but now, I hear you ask
What purpose did he have in mind?
What was his life's long task?
What venomous vision consumed him?
How would he use his technique?
Where would the dark forces lead him,
either tomorrow or maybe next week?
What was the extent of his destiny?
What was his underlying theme?
Total control leading to world domination!
Was this his ultimate dream?
A leader of a satanic world,
black hat and ceremonial robe
An empire based upon evil,
spreading across the whole globe
Happily his aims were more modest,
lacking in imaginative flair
He made himself invisible on the corpy bus,
to get out of paying the fare

Wayfinder shoes - these shoes were briefly popular in the sixties, with animal footprints shown on the sole and a 'useful' compass in the heel

Corpy bus – Liverpool slang term to describe the green 'corporation' buses

The Beer Bottle Baron of Bootle

Grey of skin and thin of face
Broken teeth, a real headcase
Monday morning he stands there
No comb ever saw his hair
Worn out shoes, each mud stained
Ashtray eyes, cheeks blood drained
Duffle bag has long been nicked
Leather casey was too well kicked
Tattered trousers old and torn
Ancient shirt with cuffs well worn
The Beer Bottle Baron of Bootle

Parents both dead, long ago
How come was that? Don't really know
His married sister, she's the boss
But doesn't really give a toss
Hot meals at night, not very much
No warmth ever, or mother's touch
Always out at late, late hours
Through hot sun or cold, cold showers
Wandering down the darkened streets
Getting cash to make ends meet
The Beer Bottle Baron of Bootle

On a wintry Sunday he's all alone
Everyone else is warm at home
The Clitheroe Kid's on the radio
But the Baron has places he needs to go
Up Orrell Road, down Rice Lane
Pub to Club and back again
Every alehouse in the region
Orange Lodge, British Legion
Prince Henry, Albert and the Plough
No one seems to notice now
Off he trails past Walton Jail
Six empties of Higson's Best Brown ale
Charlie's Chippy and the Merton

Flock wallpaper and velvet curtain
Trudging slowly past your gate
Missing out on the Welfare state
The Beer Bottle Baron of Bootle

Sing something Simple - run and hide
Before we're driven to suicide
Still the Baron's on the road
Shouldering his glassy load
Brown empties fetching much loose change
He's feeling weary, looking strange
Hears some shouts, endures some threats
'You cheeky sod!' 'Ye tight gets'
He runs away, doesn't care
A drowning rat, with soaking hair
Under the bridge of cold, hard stone
He finally sits down all alone
Counts his cash, swigs his pop
Then he strides down to the shop
Capstan full strength and matches too
Smoking's not so bad for you
Who cares too much anyway
Not him for certain anyday
The Beer Bottle Baron of Bootle

Monday morning lessons equal boredom
Homework as usual never done
Telling dirty jokes in Maths
Gets a snigger and some laughs
Father Murphy gets quite mad
'Why are you not listening lad?'
Brother Mick raises tension
'Where were you at detention?'
So he gets done once again
Arriving late home in the rain
Who cares? It's no big deal
With not one penny for a meal
The Beer Bottle Baron of Bootle

Some days enjoying massive feasts
Platefuls of leftovers from the priests
'Stay behind!' that's what they said
'Just for once you will get fed'
At a table in a warmer place
An opportunity to feed his face
How sad, but it is the truth
What a sad life for a youth
Most unpleasant and somewhat grim
The sixties never swung for him
The Beer Bottle Baron of Bootle

The Keck King

Colin was the Keck King, he wore them shiny blue
He didn't wear the grey ones, unlike me, or you
He wore them for at most a term from Easter to July
We made such endless fun of it and still I can't think why
When Spotty wore his wrangler it hardly got a mention
He only did it for a day and landed a detention
We mocked him not, soft Nape the Gape, clad in tweeds of white
but Colin the reluctant Keck King was skitted out of sight
I'd hardly have remembered him, except for that one thing
That summer term so long ago, when Colin was Keck king

Colin was the Keck King - its very sad but true
We didn't have a vote on it - we just said it's you
How we laughed and sniggered then, it really was quite cruel
But it helped to pass the time away and cope with bleeding school
It wasn't that we hated him, or had to do him down
His choice of kecks was all it took to gain that tainted crown
Every Monday morning he stood, hoping we'd forgotten
But all in vain, as once again, we'd skit him something rotten
He tried to change the subject - talk of girls or television
But his cause was always lost, we were lads with just one mission

Colin was the Keck King - of that there is no doubt
The evidence was everywhere, in every scream and shout
We called his name out in the yard and halfway up the stairs
We used to whisper quietly in post assembly prayers
Scrawling Keck King on the blackboard brought such endless joy
That daring fashion statement turned dismal for that boy
One day inside our classroom, the lad we knew as Stenno
Yelled Keck King from the window and made him miss that penno
He must have sometimes wondered when it all might end
Would a sad and bitter ex Keck King, ever find a friend?

Colin was the Keck king, back when we were fifteen
He had to grin and bare it, even though he wasn't keen
This can't be all, there must be more, things he might have done
But though in pain, I rack my brain, I can't remember one
A term it was, or thereabouts, not such a lengthy reign
The kecks then quickly vanished and were never seen again
The first day of the autumn term saw him abdicate
In brand new standard grey kecks, he stood posing at the gate
Jim Coughlan had replaced him with new, spectacular kecks
Dead tight and sandy coloured, and covered with bright checks

Colin was the Keck king, that's it, no more, no less
And as for what he's doing now, I really couldn't guess
Somehow when I think of him, it turns my thoughts quite sour
To once have been the Keck King, was that his finest hour?
Perhaps he's quite successful, or at least just getting by
His clothing quite appropriate, like any normal guy
The story of the Keck King, what really makes it worse
Is all these years later, I'm compelled to write this verse
Something drives me onward, a peculiar obsession
Like making it all public, or going to confession
And as I jot these words down, one thought comes to my head
Leave it all behind lad, be sure the Keck king did

kecks - Liverpool slang word for trousers
penno - penalty kick

The Day Out (minus the Croaker) 1969

In Ormskirk town centre we sat, beneath the old clock tower,
drinking Strongbow cider, as it chimed the midday hour.
Watching girls on lunch break pass, with certain teenage strut,
white-faced, red lipped, dark eyed, and hair, all freshly feather cut.

We nearly chatted up those two. We nearly had the nerve.
The cider gave us courage, much more than we deserved.
They both looked down their noses, as if both half asleep.
Then turned away, as if to say, "Please, just drop dead, creep."

You said it did not matter, there were plenty more besides.
Lit up a Peter Stuyvesant, inhaled and coughed and sighed.
Perhaps we'll get some flared kecks, stylish and unique.
Men of the world like Fleetwood Mac, if we find the right boutique.

Waiting for The Croaker, who never actually showed,
even though we knew full well, he'd walked down that same road.
Stumbling in the bookshop, mumbling all the while.
Anxious, flushed and twitchy, with a crooked, beaten smile.

The cider gone we sauntered, down narrow, seething streets.
The molten smells of market stalls, broken biscuits, sticky sweets,
The infants howl, the young mums whine, the Wigan boys stand hissing,
'neath drip dry shirts and plastic shoes, the entwined lovers kissing.

Much later on the Southport road, we met the cycling crew,
so self assured and purposeful in everything they do.
They had even seen The Croaker, who had talked a load of twaddle,
of Vonnegut, Heinlein and Quatermass - his usual sci-fi babble.

The sixties had five months to run, a turbulent decade.
The hacking down of old ideas, and youth the cutting blade.
But like the lunar landing, all of this seemed far away,
in Ormskirk town so long ago, on that uneventful day

Sick Will

Round up your cats, lock up your dogs
Ignore them if they howl
Put a padlock on your shed
Sick Will is on the prowl
Sick Will is a head-the-ball
He lives on our estate
He even goes to my school
Thank God he's not my mate
I only see him now and then
He's usually on his tod
I always look the other way
He's such a mental sod
Definitely more than a few bricks
short of one full hod

Sick Will sees a shrink each week
who lays him on a bed
Sick Will says he talks a bit
and looks inside his head
God knows what he finds there
I wouldn't want to see
`Cos Sick Will's brain is quite unique
All cloaked in lunacy
That's why he does the things he does
He knows no other way
His mum is at her wit's end
She says so every day

Sick Will hoards his fireworks
It ought to be a crime
And then creates urban chaos
In the long, hot summer time
The police get told of all his deeds
Sometimes they take him in
But come next day he's back again
rooting in your bin
Or roaming round with stolen paint
all plastered to his face
In a twilight zone so far removed
from all the human race

Lighting fires in the woods
at nights when weather's fine
Stealing wood from people's gardens
and washing from the line
Rides his rusty bike around
Shouts and swears all day
Makes vile gestures with his hands
People look the other way
Stands with glazed look on his face
Hanging out his tongue
Dolly Wilcox shouts at him
and says he should be hung

Watch him yokker on pedestrians
while standing on the bridge
Never ask him what he did
inside his mum's new fridge
She counts the days and counts the years
what job would suit this lad?
He wants to be a rat catcher
just like his long lost dad
But first he needs to be cured
There is no quick solution
My guess is that he'll finish up
in a very secure institution

yokker – spit
head the ball – nutcase

Morgo's Programmes

Morgo brought his footy programmes in
Not just a brief selection
But every Goodison game ever attended
His entire lifelong collection
He showed them to all and sundry
He stoppeth one in one
All agreed that his box of blue booklets
Was really second to none
He showed the dinner ladies
Who cheerfully exclaimed 'Well done!'
He recalled each and every score line
And knew who'd lost and won
He showed some of the teachers
One even cracked a smile
And actually offered to buy them
But Morgo held onto his pile

Father Gaughan was an aged priest
Infirm and often sick
He taught like a man in a coma
And was nicknamed 'Death on a Stick'
And when he came in to teach biology
Later on that autumn day
Morgo still had his programmes out
But was told to put them away
He did as bid, but five minutes later
Opened his desk one more time
Just to have a quick reshuffle
That was the extent of his crime
Gaughan called him to the front
With his programmes still clutched in his fist
He took the pile from Morgo
And then with a flick of the wrist
And a thin smile like the lid on a coffin

Steadily ripped each one in turn
You could hear a bus rumble on the distant road
As Morgo's cheeks began to burn
While shredded booklets landed in the bin
His tears began to flow
Face pressed hard against the desk lid
Seeking refuge behind his elbow
At the lessons end he retrieved the remains
And pelted off over the playing field
Next day he brought a letter in
But the outcome was never revealed
Perhaps today it would be bigger news
Headlines in the local press
Complaints to the Court of Human Rights
With Morgo seeking redress
Exhibit A – some programmes in a bag
Torn up in a burst of rage

But way back then we just thought 'Oh well!'
It was a very different age
Of course there were many who suffered much more
The episode was arguably quite trite
But even hardened Liverpool supporters
Agreed that it was sly and dead tight

The Milk Thief

On our way to school one morning
As the rain drizzled slowly down
A woman emerged from her doorway
In carpet slippers and dressing gown
Crept round to the side of her neighbour's house
Looked through the window and then bent low
Lifted a milk bottle from the doorstep
Then hurried furtively back to her home
Generously leaving the other three bottles
Perhaps they wouldn't miss one
Like stealing an egg from a bird's nest
Approach steadily, swiftly lift and be gone
Did she do it every day?
(Or maybe, just once a week)
Did she always emerge at the same time?
(Or vary her technique)
Was it for cereal, or tea and coffee?
Was there too little, or did she have plenty?
And when she'd consumed her ill gotten gains
How did she dispose of the empty?
Was she a thief in other ways?
(A shoplifter, or some kind of burglar)
Or did she have limited ambition
Choosing not to develop it further?
Perhaps it was only a one off crime
We never saw her again
Who knows? Maybe she paid it back
Unable to live with the strain
The milkman is a dying breed
Doorstep deliveries now are quite rare
People buy disposable cartons
So there may well be a statistic somewhere
Or a dossier carefully compiled
Detailing the slow and steady decline
Of milk being lifted from doorsteps
No longer a significant crime

Thorax

In Ormskirk town on Friday nights, the pubs heave forth a crowd
Of drunken lads and lasses, all singing, shouting loud
Making wisecracks, telling jokes, all shopworn even then
Trying to cadge a cig or two, from off the older men
I stood in Ormskirk bus station on one late summer's night
Way back in '71 it was, in June and still quite light
Working through a bag of chips, waiting for my bus
Keeping out of harms way, not making any fuss
A girl passed through, a striking vision, taller than the rest
Short skirted and suede booted, tight fitting granddad vest
Whistles sounded from the lads, perched on the wooden seat
And some began to follow her, as she walked along the street
Down towards the clock tower, pace quickening all the while
Ignoring catcalls and gestures, indescribably vile
'I know why they're all chasing her,' spoke one who stood alone
To no one in particular, he continued in that tone
'Have you seen the thorax on her?' he then unleashed his theory
Turning to me with bloodshot eyes, his breath, woodbined and beery
I made no riposte, but ate my chips, he helped himself as well
Then felt the need, yet again, the whole wide world to tell
'Have you seen the thorax on her?' his words hung in the air
And echoed round the bus station, as I was standing there
He spoke to all and no one, beneath the evening sky
Many must have heard him, but none did make reply
'No wonder they're all after her,' he yelled, with knowing gloat
'You should see the thorax on her', he strained his drunken throat
He spoke no more, silence resumed, a gloom fell on the station
As if we all were stunned by his unique observation
In my addled brain I tried to make some muddled kind of sense
Exactly what his point was, I really felt quite dense
Recalled my hazy, forgotten lessons in '0' level biology
Tried to visualize the concept of his chosen terminology
Did the thorax on an insect come just below the head?
Or, I thought with indecision, was that the abdomen instead?
The more I thought, the more confused I became, and even more so

His reference to her thorax, meant which part of her torso?
This strange expression that he yelled, it lingers with me still
I never heard it used that way again, perhaps I never will
I suppose when all is said and done, this is what we find
It's very strange how such a thing, becomes embedded in your mind
Those foggy misty memories, clog up your inner brain
And then come back to haunt you so many times again
To use a word like thorax in such an odd location
One Friday night, so long ago, in Ormskirk town bus station

Ormskirk New Year 1971

The clock tower signals to a waiting world, the year about to pass
And summons the youth of Ormskirk, each worthy lad and lass
Out from the Windmill and the King's Head and other drinking houses
While older ones with homes to go to, head off with their spouses
Baggy-trousered soul boys, regulars at Wigan Casino
Neatly shorn with leather brogues, Miggsy, Moxie and Deano
Stumbling girls in Crombie coats, 'Arr-eh! All the best!'
The hippy with the withered arm and tie-dyed granddad vest
Black shirts with white and glowing ties, the very latest trend
It's always great to dress up, exactly like your friend
Here comes Woofer in his greatcoat, lately gone all weird
Like a refugee from Jethro Tull, with embryonic beard
Psycho Steve from the 21 houses, sub zeroed, yet bare-chested
Dancing on a Cortina roof, about to be arrested
They bundle him into the *Black Maria*, he roars with indignation
His 15 years old fiancée gapes in admiration
Drunken Dot staggers in platform shoes, hot pants and purple maxi
Expecting and hoping against the odds, to hail a passing taxi
The clanging chimes of midnight bring forth cheers and howls
And from the over indulgent, a few contorted scowls
One or two are well tanked up, drinking since midday
Some vomit in the gutter, or piss in shop doorway
What became of those bright young things, who gathered at that time?
Older? Fatter? Balder? Wiser? Now well past their prime
No doubt a modern tribe assembles to play the annual game
Different in so many ways, yet somehow just the same
One brief moment, a mental snapshot, I can see it even now
In many ways it seems so quaint, quite innocent somehow
There's thirty years passed and gone, since I noted this strange scene
I thought I'd go back one more time, but as yet I've never been
Who knows, perhaps, I will return, when I am old and grey
To wander Ormskirk on New Years Eve and see in the following day

Black Maria – police van

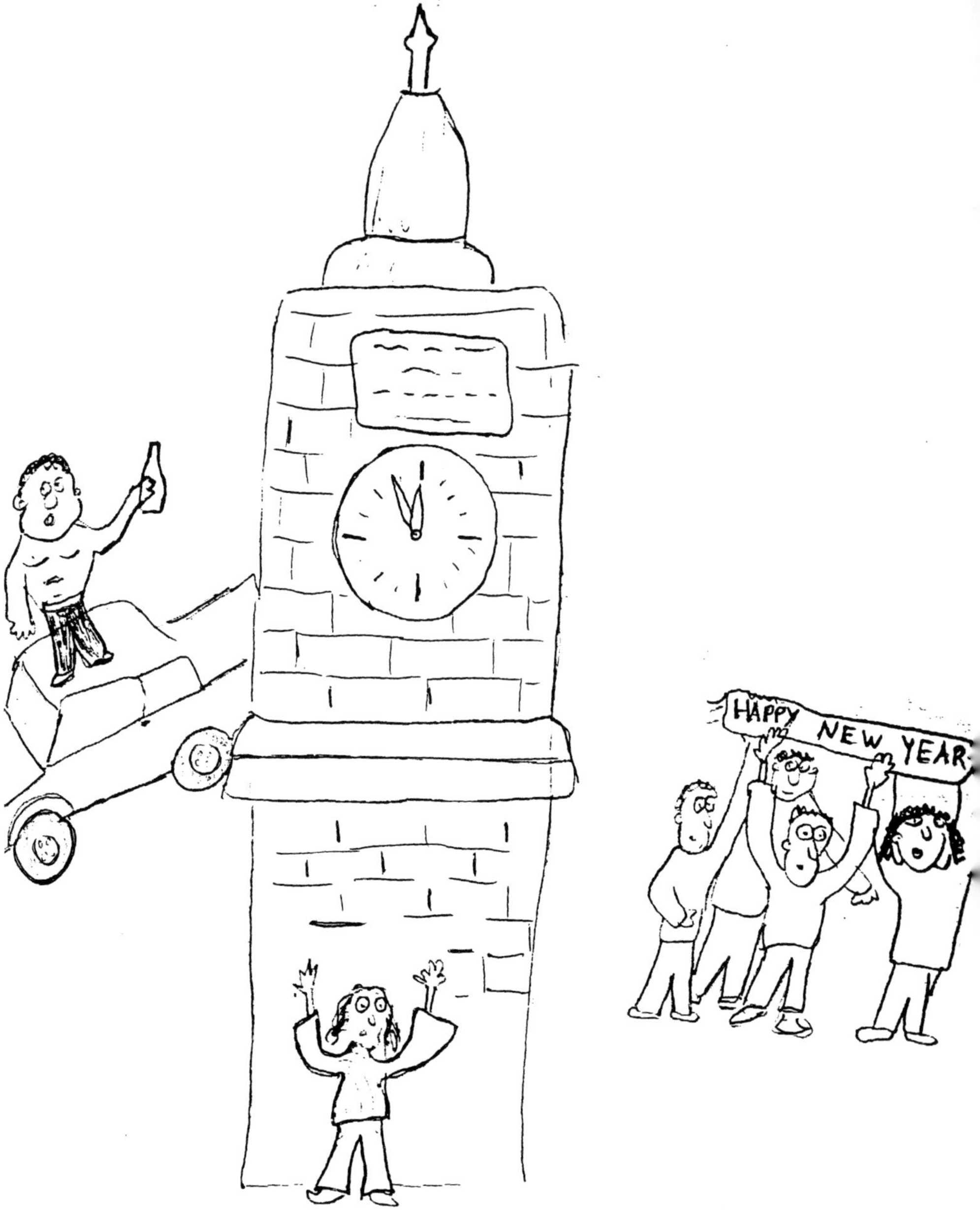
HAPPY NEW YEAR

The Plate Spinner

Wandering through Ormskirk in a youthful daze
No sense of direction or time
Deep into my own thoughts and musings
Both the past and the future in mind
With 'O' levels looming and teenage upheavals
I was feeling in so many ways low
Rambling through the municipal park
With no particular place to go

The man in a white cap and blue blazer
Pressed trousers and extremely dapper
Sought advice and assistance from me
A most sartorial shopper
He talked and there was no getting away
He wasn't in any great hurry
Not having myself any plans for the day
At that stage I felt no need to worry

He mentioned his past in the music hall
He did not dance or sing
But no doubt classed as a novelty act
Plate spinning was his thing
'I'll buy you an ice cream if you want one
Or would you like something more?'
His hand tweaked my knee as he said it
And I stared down at the floor

I didn't really want to stay
I felt inclined to disappear
Yet it seemed impolite to run away
He'd been all over Lancashire
In all his adventures across the North
He'd achieved a certain notoriety
And won over many admirers
With his capacity for variety

With nimble hands and deft footwork
And many wristly flicks
He showed me how he'd made his name
By spinning plates on sticks
Hawking his act round all the halls
Travelling by road and by rail
Appearing in every northern town
Bolton, Burnley and Rochdale

And even Clitheroe, one wet Sunday night
He'd performed with *the kid himself*
But with the music hall days well behind him
His crockery gathered dust on the shelf
He arranged to meet up the following week
And naturally I did agree
Somewhere in Southport near the Floral Hall
And then back to his place for tea

Where I could sample his porcelain set
And his imported caviar
And then rummage through his mementoes
And handle his samovar
I knew well enough what he wanted
When he said he would be my friend
I knew well enough what his game was
When he said he had money to spend

No doubt he had thespian delusions
And thought he was on to a winner
With his light footed leaping and traipsing
That superannuated, vaudevillian, plate spinner
But when the following week came around
Did I feel a strange urge to be going?
Was I anywhere at all near Southport?
With that man all winking and knowing

Captivated by his worldly ways
His hair strangely dark, but thinning
Allowing me a brief and furtive glimpse
Into the arcane world of plate spinning
Was I tempted by his greasepaint charm?
His phrases seductive and sugary
Would I venture down that weathered pier
Inevitably, perhaps? - like buggery!

The kid himself   - a reference to Jimmy Clitheroe, the diminutive entertainer from Clitheroe in Lancashire who, having established himself as the 'perpetual schoolboy in trouble' was the star of a marathon BBC Radio series 'The Clitheroe Kid' which ran from 1958 to 1972, attracting ten million listeners at its peak. He died in 1973.

Midnight Ghosts

Me and the Croaker were heading out from Ormskirk
Bored of pubs and market stalls, one Saturday late July
In search of some excitement we took the Wigan road
A warm and lazy afternoon beneath a cloudless sky
Ventured down a public footpath, though we knew not where it led
Up near the water tower, not far from Stanley Gate
Then sat beside a dry ditch as the Croaker lit a woodbine
And we shared a drop of whisky, and paused to contemplate
Then Croaker espied a paperback, recently discarded
Entitled *Midnight Ghosts*, (I don't recall the author's name)
He began to leaf through it and then he cackled loudly
I quickly snatched it from him and then did much the same
It was a pornographic tale of vice and sordid dealings
And raunchy 'goings on' detailed in nearly every page
He did this to her and she did that to him
They tore each other's clothes off in a fiery, passionate rage
Lots of frantic coupling in beds, sheds and other places
Tales of nether garments, pale skin and fishnet legs
'His manly hands slowly caressed her silken thigh'
And mysterious references to 'chapel hat pegs'
The plot was somewhat sketchy, but the descriptions very graphic
And we quickly skimmed the pages to find many that were lewd
We chose to read aloud in mock Shakespearian accent
Impersonating Richard Burton in a manner rather crude
Then we reached the road again and *Midnight Ghosts* now bored us
The cheap paperback was already fragmenting in our hands
So Croaker lobbed this sordid yarn into a field of growing barley
Knowing not and caring less, where it might choose to land
All of which is a sober reminder, to all who would be writers
That in the world of publishing, that is how it sometimes goes
The author might sit for many hours producing worthy fiction
But what eventually becomes of it he never really knows
His work might end its days on a crammed suburban bookshelf
Between travel guide and car manual, slowly gathering dust

Or tossed like *Midnight Ghosts* into an open field of barley
That un-inspirational tale of depravity and lust
Churned up during late August by a hired combined harvester
Never to be perused again, by youthful eyes no more
That shredding of such fiction seemed somehow rather fitting
Absorbed back into nature, inside a bale of straw

The Lakes

When winter comes and brings the frost and ice
Some people opt to pay a heavy price
They like to have a worthwhile risk to take
Desiring to tread across a frozen lake
Eventually they will hear a cracking sound
And inevitably some of them are drowned

When summer comes and days are sticky and hot
One or two will always lose the plot
Plunging into any handy reservoir
Ignoring all the dangers that are there
Yet again it's no way to behave
Unless you're longing for a watery grave

Then relatives all start to whinge and whine
Demanding instant action at the time
People must be very carefully protected
Fences and signs must hastily be erected
But you cannot treat the public like a newborn kitten
Nor can you fence off every lake in Britain

And if someone chooses to walk down a railway line
Listening to his walk-man at the time
Again he should not be entirely surprised
If the 6.15 appears and cuts him down to size
This point may seem a little harsh and cruel
But you cannot always intercept the fool

The more barriers and protections that you make
The greater the risks they'll be inclined to take
The end result is always much the same
There must be someone else to take the blame
In short, this point I feel has some validity
You cannot protect the moron from his own stupidity

Lunch Break-up
I had tentatively arranged to meet you
At the start of your lunch hour
Around the point of midday
We would meet under the clock tower
I got there just after half ten
And wandered from pillar to post
Checking out 45s on the market
And buying the two I liked most
In some ways I felt rather lonely
In others I felt just alone
In a strange way I knew what would happen
The seeds had already been sown
You emerged from the shop doorway
And headed off down the street
Unaware of my presence behind you
The one you expected to meet
Your coat worked its way through the crowd
All I needed to do was call
But yet I stood like a statue
I didn't do anything at all

I slipped away from the public
Found a place where I could hide
Being true to myself for a short while
Better this than to have lied
Out in the park on a hard bench
I gave myself a talking to
Resolving to be more decisive
It was high time to follow through
This relationship was now in the descendent
I needed to be on my own
The final details did not matter
As this chain of events had just shown

Sometimes you must take it slowly
And give yourself time to think
Avoiding all lunchtime meetings
No pale pasty or coffee to drink
No prolonged and awkward pauses
No tearful inquisition
No need for me to stay calm
Or restate my position

I heard the end of your lunch break
I heard the clock tower chime
And I knew for certain that you and me
Were finished for good this time

Dyslexia

The land they call Dyslexia
Isn't very big
None of the people can spell too well
Except for the man who is *Knig*

The Walton Wedding

Uncle Frank is full of ale
Driving guests around the twist
Matching partners to get up and dance
Working through a mental list
Daft Bob is as daft as a brush
He's spilt his pint again
Eddie's mates have told him
To be home by half past ten
Jimmy Johnno dances with Auntie Marge
His wife is holding forth
On matters relating to modern art
As always a total bore
The ale flows like a river
The disco booms loud and long
The girls from work dance their legs off
To *Tainted Love* and *the Birdie Song*
Wearing clothes they've all bought special
Dresses short and tight
From Maureen Murphy's catalogue
To celebrate this night
Uncle Billy sits and gives it out
About a life on British Rail
Teenage son sits in seething silence
Countenance vacant and pale
Leaving school with no qualifications
Not outstanding or clever
Ahead a lifetime of casual labour
And much futile endeavour
Uncle Gerry's banging on the table
And singing Johnny Cash
Auntie Claire just sits and stares
At a tray that's full of ash
Auntie Nora is flirting still
Although she's fifty eight

Chairman Bernie's heard to say
She's left it rather late
Our Joe's mates have just gate-crashed
They're keeping out of sight
Cousin Tommy has his shirt off
And he's looking for a fight
A few hours of madness months in planning
All gone in the wink of an eye
Leaving stains, hangovers and empty wallets
And one more tear to cry
Chairman Bernie sniffs the empties
Noticing who's drunk what
The teetotal crew from the Wirral
Have put away quite a lot
The bride is big but not as yet
As fat as she is going to be
The groom is as thin as a starving crow
(His thyroid apparently)
This man and wife will venture forth
And be happy for a year or two
One decade and three kids later
Their divorce was coming through
He ran off with an older woman
Who drives a camper van
She met a lonely bloke called Baz
Some kind of dairyman
That was the wedding in Walton
The years have been and gone
So much has changed in so many ways
Since that night in eighty one

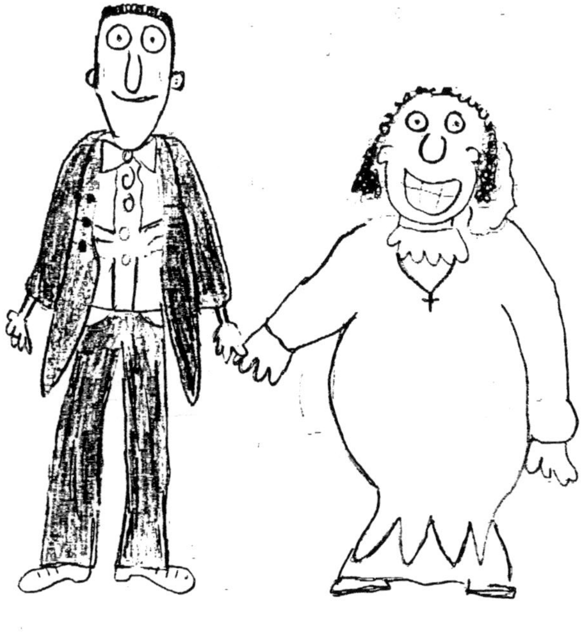

The Shadow Boxer

He entered the pub with his coated wife
Fretfully following behind
Ordered a pint and a glass of stout
A man with a mission in mind
Sat at a table to the side of the dartboard
Lit up and emitted a cough
Three pints later he stood abruptly
And slowly took his shirt off
Loose fitting trousers with fists held high
Sporting a plain grey vest
Eagerly anticipating the round one bell
Ready to fight a clean contest

Some stared, some looked the other way
But none did intervene
As he stood his ground and traded punches
With an enemy unseen
He landed jabs in the solid, smoking air
Keeping his chin tucked in
Practising his shuffle, bobbing and weaving
Like they trained him in the gym
Before him, misty memories of his finest hours
Of battles long and hard
A handful of wins, some close defeats
At Liverpool stadium on the undercard

He fought a close three rounder
Landing punches with precision
And then shook hands with each of us
After he'd got the decision
Another drink then before the fading sun
Gives way to the darker night
Shirt on once more and out he went
To face the hardest fight
His wife close behind in his footsteps
More faithful than a dog
As they journey onward together
Through the smouldering, thickening fog

The Last Taxi ride

I met him and his wife in Ormskirk bus station
On the night the last bus never showed
I'd been to see a film in the local Pavilion
They'd been in The Windmill on Wigan Road
We were going the same way, so we flagged down a taxi
She said they should get out a bit more
He said he was currently between one job and another
But something would turn up, he was sure
And he was quite reluctant to let me pay my share
When I insisted, he slowly relented
At that stage no sign of a dark, troubled mind
Or a man inwardly tormented
The Advertiser headlined his passing
Highlighting the doom and the gloom
In his garage with his car and a hosepipe
A death caused by poisonous fumes
And I thought long about our last meeting
Searching hard for some tell-tale sign
And yet there was nothing, he'd seemed easy going
And in many ways gentle and kind
No one is suicidal until they become so
The mind is ever inclined to pirouette
The black mist can engulf you without any warning
And drag you down to dark despair and deep regret
His wife and three children attended his funeral
Rain fell as they all stood and cried
Could anyone have foreseen this ill-fated out-come
On the night of the last taxi ride?

Gobbed in Town

The blues had won their final game
Escaping the dread relegation
And so he was out to enjoy the night
Intent on intoxication
In his threadbare suit with fraying cuffs
And lapels a shade too wide
He was a man on a mission to drink
Nothing less would have satisfied
With blotchy face and dodgy perm
Inside his favourite boozer
His opinionated views on life
Marked him out as a loser
He would always be the last to notice
Exactly what was going down
But this would be a night to remember
When he got *gobbed in town*

He argued the toss about the footy
Said Shankly was just crap
And only someone who was mental
Would ever set foot in the Kop
Roger Hunt was never the legend
That he was always cracked up to be
Big Ron Yeats was just a yard dog
As anyone could easily see
None were worthy to lick the boots
Of Alex Young, *the golden vision*
These and other views of life
Brought forth howls of derision
And yet no one seemed too bothered
As he called for one more round
This was an evening to celebrate
The night he was *gobbed in town*

Catterick took over from Carey of course
Post infamous taxi ride
The blues were unassailable then
He'd worn his scarf with pride
Started recalling the Cavern club
Those halcyon sixties days
Drink was cheap and girls were willing
It was all a wondrous haze
'The Beatles!' he uttered, sacrilegiously
'Not a patch on The Big Three'
Of course he had known the drummer
And used to see them for free
And he was a mate of the DJ
Back in that glorious decade
When life had so much more on offer
And his Carnaby Street gear wasn't frayed
Then he stumbled off to the bog once more
After swilling three chasers down
Well and truly off his head
The night he was *gobbed in town*

He should never have mentioned *Our Cilla*
That was his big downfall
Claiming carnal knowledge of the diva
Outside near the cavern wall
Out from the corner stepped a man
Who took a manly stride
Built like a breezeblock bogshed
With shoulders implausibly wide
'I'll have you know she's my auntie,' says he
As the crowd all cleared a space
Then grabbing him by the flock décor
He stared right into his face
Then banged his head against the wall
Some six or seven times
He began to pay a heavy price
For all his mouthy crimes

Down he fell, the pub was hushed
No one said a word
Some thought he had it coming
And most could not have cared
Seized by the ornate portals
He met the pavement with a bang
Leaving behind that cosy tavern
At the moment last orders rang
Blood flowed down his chalk-stripe suit
And mingled with the rain
Numbed by copious alcohol
He hardly felt the pain
As he stared into the gutter
Left to slowly drown
His last thoughts before a deep, deep sleep-
I've just been *gobbed in town*

This tale of commonsense is told
A warning to one and all
When you hit the town and bottle
Be careful whom you call
Mouth off about footballing legends
And the Beatles, if you're a nutter
But don't besmirch the name of *Cilla*
Or you'll end up snogging the gutter

Mental in the Fens

Land of pastures so serene
A quaint and pleasant rural scene
The flattest place I've ever been
Never forgotten once its seen
Sky looms down on horizons clean
No hills or valleys in between
Home to boxing legend, Dave 'Boy' Green
The *Fen Tiger*, lean and keen
Solitary farmers daily toil
Where generations have worked the soil
Eggs to fry and fowl to boil
This is the Fen country

I went down to the Fen country
To enjoy a weekend away
To a peaceful market town I came
An idyllic place to stay
Intent on mingling with the locals
Those rustic farming chaps
Full of ancient wisdom and homespun truths
Comical yarns of agrarian mishaps
Gazing across the village green
Observing a bygone age
Watching games of bowls and cricket
Turning back history's page

On Friday night the town got full
Of lusty young farming types
Working their way round all three pubs
Getting tanked up for the night
They scarcely knew restraint at all
As they came in from the Fens
Carrot farmers and poultry producers
Well acquainted with geese and hens

Centuries of inbreeding had left them
Dim and ineffectual
If you can breathe with your mouth shut tight
They call you an intellectual
Lantern jawed and hollow cheeked
Vacant in the eye
Ready for a good night out
Passions running high
I heard two fellows start a fight
One said to the other, 'Hey mister!
I hear you're marrying your first cousin
What's wrong with your sister?'
He said 'Don't be so bleedin'stupid
You country bumpkin lad
You know I can't get married to her
She's already wed - to my dad'
I met another in a pub doorway
His eyes lit up with glee
He said 'you're not from round these parts
You're not like him or me'
He set about me with his fists
I hastily ran away
Pursued by a mob of mentalists
Keen to join in the affray
Police were nowhere to be seen
As they landed blows and kicks
Some had come forewarned and armed
And brandished sturdy sticks
I made no sound and lay on the ground
Pretending to be dead
For all I knew that might be soon
As blood poured from my head
At last the youths got bored and left
Looking for others to attack
Making triumphant gurgling noises
While I lay on my back

I crawled slowly across the dismal street
My expression sore and pained
A kindly old man paused to helpfully proclaim
'You've been gobbed, battered and brained''

The rosy-cheeked landlady
Tended to my wounds
She said, 'If I were you my lad
I 'd go home very soon'
I went down to the Fen country
It wasn't up to much
I entered town with my head held high
And clumped out on a crutch
I gazed back with a jaundiced view
Of flattened fields and ditches
I could only stare with my right eye
The left was closed with stitches
Limping back through Leeds again
The people seemed kind and gentle
I'm not going back to the Fen country
They're all too bleedin' mental

The Timelord

I want to be a Timelord
A latter day Doctor Who
Travelling through many dimensions
With a very singular crew
A glamorous and helpful companion
Short skirt and wide trusting eyes
Would help me to deal with all dangers
And ever be there at my side
Negotiating final frontiers
As we journey through space and through time
When I rescue her from the Daleks
I know she would always be mine
We'd see off the sinister Cybermen
Blow out the Zarbis as well
I'd make wisecracks and acerbic comments
And watch her fall under my spell
We'd drink nectar while encircling Neptune
We'd feast on a Saturnian moon
Then jive to a Jovian jukebox
Pumping out a Plutonian tune
Alone at last in the Tardis
I'd turn the flashing lights low
Take a break from conserving the Cosmos
And make love for a light year or so

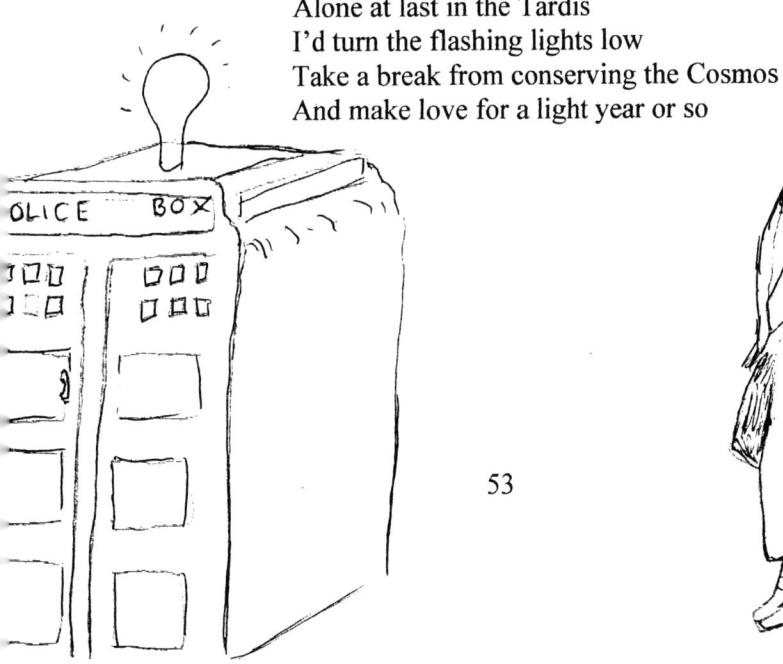

The Middling Muddling Years

When I was young I used to dread what middle age might bring
'Hope I die before I get old,' was the song I used to sing
People over thirty lived such sad and dreary lives
Vacuous boring husbands and shrewish nagging wives
Sitting in a rocking chair, cursing all the vandals
Looking so lounge lizard like, blue socks with brown sandals
The Daily Mail was usually read, with predictable, political prescription
And letters to the editor about bringing back conscription

Never going out too much, slumped in front of screen
Watching variety programmes, better left unseen
Sunday Night at the London Palladium, Black and White Minstrel Show
The Good Old Days with Leonard Sachs, 'Ha ha! Hee hee! Ho ho!'
Buying tedious outfits from Greenwood the tailor in town
Tweed jackets and woolly jumpers in grey or beige or brown
A collection of bri-nylon shirts, white for Sunday best
Lots of baggy Y fronts and obligatory string vest

Women in voluminous dresses, headscarves like big towels
Discussing all their ailments, the workings of their bowels
Female underwear back then would make a lad's blood curdle
Sturdy foundation garments, a tightly fastened girdle
Corsets held together, many hooks and complex clips
Ready to face the waiting world with pinched and bloodless lips
In summer on a crowded coach, heading to the beach
Sit with hanky on your head, fish-paste baps in easy reach

Boring salads on a Sunday, spring onions and corned beef
Slices of beetroot, bits of egg, a watery lettuce leaf
Listening to *Sing Something Simple*, a Sunday night fixation
Planning a night in a Berni Inn – a birthday celebration
A portrait of that Spanish girl, above the fireplace
Stand proud in your carpet slippers as you stare into her face
Surround yourself with ornaments – bits of useless brass
Sleeping on candy-striped, terylene sheets, false teeth placed in a glass

Hating all the young ones, despising their youth and hair
Complaining about their music, and the clothes that they all wear
Well, here I am at a certain age, with thirty long since gone
Recordings by James Last and such – as yet I haven't one
No teasmade or hostess trolley, no love of Variety
The bigot in a basket circuit isn't yet for me
The things that I have always done, I still quite like to do
Though I will admit I listen now, much more to Radio 2

Forty, I'm reliably informed, is now the new twenty-one
And fifty is the new thirty, so don't think you're getting on
And here's the new philosophy, the latest phrase to quote is
'Middle age has been deferred until further notice'
And if the bright young things suggest we might have made a blunder
Feeling aggrieved at our middle youth, since we stole all their thunder
Don't marginalize or isolate them, don't leave them in the lurch
Just pen a letter to the Daily Mail – let's bring back the birch!'

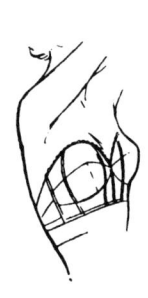

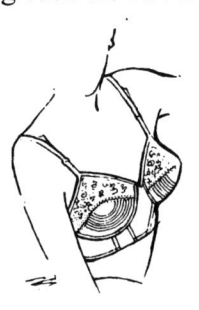

The disproportionately large-busted woman must call upon the aid of her corsetière and her dressmaker. For a brassiere built to fit a particular figure problem will minimize it to a certain extent, helping to smooth out and re-distribute the flesh to give the figure a better-proportioned look.

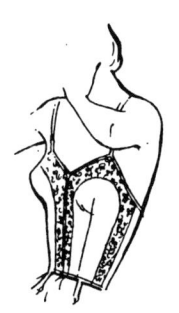

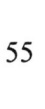

(Source *'How To Keep Your Figure'* pub. **Housewife** 1953

Puerto Rican boxer Wilfred Benitez was, at seventeen, the youngest man ever to win a world championship in professional boxing. In total he was a world champion in three different weight categories. This poem tells of his sad decline.

Wilfred Benitez

Wilfred Benitez turned professional when he was just fifteen
Rising quickly up the ratings with a speed that's rarely seen
His achievements were soon chronicled on every sporting page
When he won his first world title at seventeen years of age
Slipping punches with radar skill, hard to hit with precision
Ready to take on the very best in more than one division
Moving up through weight categories, winning two more crowns
The pride of Puerto Rico, a hard man to put down
Leonard, Hearns, Duran he fought them all, the brightest of the era
But by his middle twenties, the end was getting nearer
The reflexes no longer quite so fast, his skills began to fade
Along with any evidence of the money that he made
Soon to be a spent force, a journeyman, windblown
For younger, hungry fighters, a useful stepping stone
Somewhere in Canada, at thirty-two, he lost his final fight,
And even those not in the know sensed that things weren't right
Advised to take a neurological test, but Wilfred didn't bother
He caught a plane to Puerto Rico, returning home forever
Unaware at that time of his dismal, impending fate
Collapsing in his own home at the age of thirty eight
An inflamation of the brain was the medical description
But sadly not available yet is any effective prescription
Dementia pugilistica was what the experts said
A very likely consequence of punches to the head
This man who was a treble champion, with arrogance and style
In a room that daylight never sees, sits now with wistful smile
Destined to live in a twilight world, not allowed to roam
Unable if he does so to find his way back home
He can't control his movements, he finds it hard to speak
His condition deteriorating with every passing week

His wife and home have disappeared, his furniture hauled away
The eight million dollars earned in the ring, long since gone astray
His existence now dependent on a loving mothers care
No sign of the bloodsucking leeches, who helped to place him there
So, young men who would aspire to make a living with your fists
Before you sign your life away, take note of all the risks
Broken noses can be straightened, you'll soon forget the pain
But rather more enduring is the damage to your brain
Hear the story of Wilfred Benitez, familiar, tragic and true
And pray you're not beyond repair when the glory days are through

May 23rd 1981 Wilfred Benitez – former light welterweight and welterweight champion captures light middleweight championship from Britain's Maurice Hope

No Ribbons Needed

They were not actors, they were not stars
No fancy clothing, no flashy cars
No wheel of fortune would turn their way
The best on offer was yesterday
Their streets were never paved with gold
Just lines of housing, bought and sold
With a white dust blowing, both night and day
In places where the children play

Beside the fail school, as light did fade
The dust was gathered and games were played
Pick up a handful, by the redbrick wall
Like snow in springtime you watch it fall
You did not know then, your fate was sealed
By a poison cloud, not yet revealed
No warnings given, no mothers knew
The pain their children, would all go through

And they will walk, a slow, slow walk
Down a one way street, with no return
Each breath comes slowly, and words are few
Dull eyes will water, and lungs will burn
No ribbons needed, no speeches made
No recognition of the price they paid
No concerts playing, for those who died
A hard luck story, from the other side

A slow death waiting, a lengthy fuse
A painful ending, a life to lose
And what of those, who caused this crime?
They slip away like the sands of time

Vanessa's Thong

Vanessa's quite a big girl now, she takes size twenty-six
All the diets failed to work, she's like a bag of bricks
Her clothes are all too tight, she feels sad all the time
Even though she tells herself being fat is not a crime
Her husband doesn't love her now, he keeps himself alone
Stays in and surfs the internet, when he has to be at home
Plans trips to foreign places that cost at least three grand
Says he has to 'find himself' in some exotic land
The kids are hyper active and so she shouts and screams
Which only makes them worse, at least that's how it seems
And so she smokes some more cigs, which make her chest feel tight
And regrets the fact that Gary never shows his face at night
She thinks of all those distant days when she was young and slim
Pursued by lots of eager men, but the one she chose was him
He didn't have those tattoos then, his teeth were still quite white
But now they're brown from smoking which he does both day and night
All they seem to do is row about the kids, the house, the jeep
The debts upon the credit cards that never let her sleep
In vain she sits and wonders when and why it all went wrong
And then she had the bright idea to buy herself a thong
They come in bigger sizes, so perhaps in shiny black
When Gary gets to know of this he'll soon come running back
Forget about the overtime, ignore computer games
Up to bed they'll quickly go and hide themselves away
Fall back in love just like before with kisses and with hugs
Roll upon the bedroom floor among the sheepskin rugs
Afterwards just sit and talk about their future plans and schemes
A lifetime shared together with many hopes and dreams
She puts on her see through nightie, showing all she's got
A chest size forty - double D adds up to quite a lot
Sits up and waits for Gary to come home from the pub
Asks him if he'd like her to give his back a rub
Slips on his favourite music, they listen to their song
Then she reveals her purchase - the sexy, brand new thong
She says they're all the rage now, the very latest fashion
Guaranteed to cause a spark, ignite forgotten passion
Reluctant Gary strokes her hair, then leans across to kiss her
And stirs the dying embers of his love for poor Vanessa

The Tattooed Lady's Son

In the class a whippet faced lad, always sitting near the back
In many ways strange - not the full quid
Usually up to something in a low cunning kind of way
Peculiar and unsettled - a weird sort of kid
The tattooed lady's son

Doing our paperback reader, girls would soon be grumbling
About his grunting noises and twitching roaming hands
Out cross-country running, legs moving like a traction engine
Came in eventually - breathing in short suspicious gasps
The tattooed lady's son

Sometimes we had a go at him, other times we just ignored him
Now and then we'd laugh at him, until the tears did flow
Sometimes he could turn nasty, get real red faced and angry
Turn snarly and scratchy and tell us where to go
The tattooed lady's son

She came in once complaining that her son was treated badly
She said he didn't get a fair chance, (or a crack of the whip!)
We caught a rare glimpse of exotic cobras and Chinese dragons
But he pretended not to know her, tight dress, red lipped – (his mum!)
The tattooed lady's son

Mad Lap Dancing Woman (the curse of Ceaucescu)

On a lads night out, having drank quite a few
A strange woman materialized
Keen to discuss a wide range of topics
She was difficult to categorize
I thought 'Oh well, fair enough, let's go!'
And expounded my wisdom at length
She was, apparently, an enthusiast of film noir
Not perhaps my particular strength
But I did my best and held my own
And then suddenly she started singing
Selected examples of Bulgarian ballads
Which set alarm bells ringing
And yet I remained lethargically languid
Not desiring to create any commotion
Found space for another pint or two
Tried hard not to show any emotion
She went on about this and also that
Quoting literature somewhat obscure
Asked if I was a fan of Jack Wladek
I replied that I wasn't quite sure

She said she worked in a massage parlour
And became even more animated
Exposing to me her business card
All smooth and laminated
Services of a very personal nature
Appeared to be her forte
It was becoming increasingly plain to me
She was more than a little bit naughty
And then on certain weekday evenings
Just to fill the vacant void
As a late nightclub lap dancer
She was gainfully employed

My mates were all getting twitchy
And glancing towards the door
It was time to head to the curry house
Like so many times before
'Ok,' she said, 'I'll come along,
I haven't eaten yet'
I said, 'I don't think that's really wise,
After all we've not long met.'

She followed through and there we sat
She on my right hand side
Getting louder with each minute
And me wishing I could hide
Flirting with all the lads as well
Behaving quite outrageous
And them just looking at each other
As if she was contagious
She seized a waiter by the scented candle
Demonstrating one of her tricks
And all the while she was holding forth
On east European politics
'Ceauscescu!' I opined without prior thought
'A jumped up Romanian cobbler'
And for reasons destined to remain unexplained
At this she threw a wobbler

'What the hell would you know?'
With hands outstretched she yelled
And then she got quite physical
And poor fat Phil was felled
By an uppercut to his jawbone
Which sent him quickly sprawling
The diners watched in silence
It was shameful and appalling
She pulled the tablecloth across

Spilling quantities of food and beer
Poppadoms propelled into orbit
While she just stood and sneered
Her scowls and howls would indicate
Some brain cells gone quite faulty
And desperate Dave was covered in
A carefully chosen balti
My beloved green linen jacket
Was suddenly all awash
With chunks of chicken korma
And bits of rogan josh
Mick had worn his brand new shirt
In truth he was a poser
But now stood plastered with pilau rice
And vegetable somoza
She screamed and bawled blue murder
Her face had turned quite red
We calmed her down eventually
By pouring beer on her head
Then bundled her out of that curry house
Into a waiting taxi cab
Pleading 'Please take this woman home,
And we'll pick up the tab'

We apologized profusely and then we left
Well and truly traumatized
There was no two ways about it
We'd been bloody Balkanized
So now I spend my life in fear
Of women who work in fleshpots
Studiously avoiding discussions
About dead Romanian despots
I can't go back to that curry house
My face and name they know it
Bring on the mad lap-dancing girl
Exit Raftery the poet

Dad

I got pregnant at fifteen, it wasn't meant to be
But these things happen, as you know, and sadly then to me
At first it was a secret I didn't dare to mention
But pretty soon I found myself the centre of attention
My mum she cried, my dad went mad, and said 'What is his name?'
I said his name was Darren, but we were both to blame
One day I was a schoolgirl, chewing gum and being bored
But come round to exam time I was in the labour ward
A girl born slightly premature, but normal so they said
And then I named her Kylie and she was bottle-fed

I brought her home, my mum helped out and showed me what to do
I soon got used to sleepless nights and the stinky smell of poo
My mates all seemed quite jealous when they came round to call
With little fluffy toys and boots and pictures for the wall
They all took turns to hold her and listen to me moan
And all agreed that, in a way, I was now almost grown
Julie said she'd like one too, and Tracey said – 'One day!'
But first they'd like to live a bit and I just turned away
And then they said they had to go, they had a wild night planned
I said 'OK I'll see you soon,' as Kylie bit my hand

Darren the dad comes round as well, we're really going steady
He says we will get married, when we're good and ready
He plays forward for the footy team, he's got a winning smile
He plans to get a good job, but not yet for a while
He's got to get GNVQs, he's quite a clever lad
With a smart gold ring from Argos that bears the legend *Dad*
He takes Kylie at weekends and leaves her with his mum
When he goes clubbing with his mates and having lots of fun
But still I do believe him when he tells me we'll get wed
'On a beach in Benidorm or some such place,' he said

Years have passed and Kylie's grown and Darren's long since gone
'It probably wasn't meant to be,' he said, the day that he moved on
My mates all got quite good jobs and some earn quite good pay
In London, York and Manchester and places far away
But life goes on the way it does, sometimes it's drab and sad
You mustn't plan too far ahead, it only drives you mad
And me I do some cleaning, which leaves my brain quite numb
And dream about the plans I made before I was a mum
My daughters gone the same way, she's just been for a scan
I wonder if Argos do a ring that bears the legend *Gran*

Sharon and Karen, Shane and Wayne (a.k.a. The Kids From Fame)

Outside the pub one Friday night
Shane and Wayne got up to fight
Going at it hammer and tongs
Jab! Cross! Jab! Bing! Bang! Bong!
A small crowd stood looking on
A barman rang for a police van
Girlfriend Sharon went in the pub
Drank her lager, Glub! Glub! Glub!
A hefty lass, weighing fifteen stone
On account of how she was big boned
Sang karaoke – a song called Fame
Said everyone would know her name
Dancing with her arms held high
People would see her, then they'd die

Girlfriend Karen, skinny and lean
Tried frantically to intervene
Without hesitation she waded in
Eight stone three of bone and skin
Baby tucked beneath one arm
As she desperately appealed for calm
They took no heed, increased the pace
And one punch landed in her face
She fled as blood poured from her nose
Dripping on the baby as he dozed
Oblivious to all the aggravation
His mother howling with consternation
Then allowing herself a watery grin
As boyfriend Wayne began to win

Big Sharon then came on the scene
Quite animated she began to scream

Boyfriend Shane was getting pasted
Taken apart, being lambasted
She dived quickly on the other bloke
Grabbed his neck, he began to choke
His knees buckled as he went down
With a heavy thud he hit the ground
His life flashed by, for what it's worth
He began to resemble an ailing smurf
But a police van then came into view
And up the path two coppers flew
Dragged off big Sharon nice and quick
And hauled them off to the local nick

At the Magistrates Court the following week
They were all disinclined to speak
Done for causing an affray
But living to fight again some day
Best friends again, blame was shared
With a hefty fine and an angry word
Local gazette printed all their names
A minor triumph for the kids from fame
But the pub landlord had marked their card
For at least a year they were all barred
You don't need talent to be in the news
Just have a scrap when you're on the booze
Enjoy the recognition while you can
Your fifteen minutes will soon be gone

The Incredible Suntanned Woman

I've seen her on her way to work
She is fairly tall and thin
On wintry mornings she gives off a glow
Caused by her orange skin
She owns a sun-bed I would guess
And uses it every day
And so she shines from head to foot
In an effervescent way
Like a Belisha beacon in overload
Or a mobile hazard warning
Or a traffic light stuck on amber
To illuminate your morning
An enlarged nectarine overfed
Or genetically modified
A satsuma grown in a laboratory
Or an egg that's over-fried
Perhaps one day I'll chat to her
Find out what makes her tick
Maybe I'll get to know her better
That radiating chick
Perhaps one day our lips will meet
Inside I will explode
And then I'll finally get to know
How it feels ….. to be tangoed!

Smart Boy Wanted

A rambling boy in search of employment
Came to a humdrum northern town
Any old job would suffice for a while
To bring in a few precious pounds
A sign in a doorway caught his darting eye
But he felt confused and affronted
For it gave little clue as to what was required
Stating simply that a *smart boy* was wanted

But what is a smart boy when all's said and done?
What qualities should a smart boy possess?
Does it concern his cranial capacity?
Or refer more to how he is dressed?
He thought about this as he stood there
And considered what it might mean
What the future might hold for a smart boy
If the smart boy was eager and keen

Because smart boys march to a different drum
They hark to the tick and the tock
They dance to the sound of a muffled pipe
And work to the beat of the clock
And smart boys like to ring changes
They know how to move and to shake
Incessantly, upwardly mobile
Smart boys must be on the make

And smart boys wear brogues all spick and all span
And striped shirts with button down collars
A thousand quid is defined as a grand
And pounds get converted to dollars
Their watches cost more than your average Joe
Their car is a source of great pride
They seek houses with very neat gardens
And exquisite kitchens inside

And smart boys impress the office girls
Not so confident or as self-assured
Who drink martini and vodka with lime
All coiffeured and well manicured
And smart boys will put in the hours
They know how to strike a good deal
Doing business with an inscrutable smile
And never reveal what they feel

They run their lives like a well-oiled machine
Never pausing to ever ask why
Work their whole lives for a gold-watch and chain
Then clock off and go home to die
And when the dust has all settled
When the smart boy has served out his time
Does the world really notice much difference?
When the smart boy has gone down the line

And seeing what lay in the future
That wandering boy felt downhearted
He turned around in the doorway
And said,'It is time I departed'
He stood and stared at the sign once more
Staggered into the street and then ranted
To a largely indifferent and uncaring world
'I'll not be a *smart boy wanted*'

Holiday in Yarmouth

'Where did you go on your holidays Keith?'
I heard the ancient glass collector ask.
As Keith stood slowly washing his hands,
Having completed his urinatory task
He swayed very slightly, then stood and stared,
As if needing to ponder the question
Began at last to enunciate his reply,
Which he did with some hesitation.
'Yarmouth!' he spoke in a voice harsh and clipped,
As if it cost money to speak.
Conveying at once both contempt and loathing,
For the place where he'd spent a whole week
'What was the weather like?' persisted the old man,
'Did it rain or did it stay fine?'
'I don't know,' replied Keith very promptly
'I was *in the alehouse all the time*'

In the alehouse all the time, now could that ever be?
The strangest way to spend your days on holiday by the sea
No silent stroll in the afternoon, along the golden sand
No whispered conversations, with a loved one hand in hand
No coastal walks or picnics, no futile fishing trips
No ice cream, or fizzy pop, to wash down your fish and chips
No collecting shells, or paddling and no mad donkey rides
No kiss me quick hats in the rain, or helter-skelter slides
No candyfloss, or sticks of rock, or postcards sent back home
No visible reason why at all he ever bothered to roam

In the alehouse all the time, now is that all he did?
Downing endless pints and spirits and from the world well hid
No doubt he stayed somewhere at least, a place for bed and board
A landlady given to whining about holidays abroad
Leaving the pub at closing time and heading for his bed
Awake the following morning, swollen tongue and pounding head
A late breakfast, a tabloid-scan, then head off once again
Collar high, head bowed low, come sun, or wind, or rain
Only springing into life, when in his favourite place
The years of heavy drinking, now etched upon his face

In the alehouse all the time, a statement hard to credit
I would ruminate on the rationale of anyone who said it
Perhaps his image was at stake, a most rambunctious lad
Hell bent on self-promotion, hard drinking bad and mad
In his mind, maybe he outlined, an alternative scenario
A man of the world, a 'jack the lad', a bus stop lothario
A charmer with a slurring speech, ready if not always able
But ever willing to have a go and drink you under the table
One for the ladies, a latter day rake, straight from a magazine
Amorous and adventurous, a self styled libertine

    My reflections on this issue came at last,
    to a sudden and abrupt end
    The glass collector turned to me,
    as if to a long lost friend
    Then he whispered most conspiratorially,
    with singular preoccupation
    His eyes glowed with the insight
    of a man with a profound revelation
    'You'd know what the weather would be like,'
    Was his telling point of view
    'You could look up at the window and see
    the sun come shining through.
    You couldn't just not know at all
    You would have some idea
    Otherwise, why go anywhere?
    You might as well stay here.'
    I felt no need a word to utter
    I had nothing left to state
    His wisdom needed no reply
    It was beyond debate
    I'd like to think there was a deeper meaning
    Something worthy of recall
    But after due consideration
    There is, quite sadly, bugger all

The Tight Get

He buys his kecks from Cheaptex
Two for the price of one
His socks are just a size too tight
He strains to get them on
He goes down town to buy his shoes
All cheap and made of plastic
His undies are all full of holes
And lacking in elastic
His shirts are made of nylon
Which makes him scratch and sweat
But never does he give a toss
'Cos he is *one tight get*

His tightness is a legend
At work he is notorious
He scrimps and saves the whole day
In a manner quite laborious
Recycles rusty paper clips
Nicks tippex when he can
Eats all the left over sarnies
Stale cheese and dried up ham
Takes plastic spoons and sugar cubes
And sachets of red sauce
On spying drawing pins in walls
Removes them with brute force

At nights he goes out to a pub
But not one that is near
He strides to one two miles away
Saves tuppence on the beer
When it comes round to Christmas time
He hides himself away
Not giving or receiving

It's far too much to pay
To be as tight as the tight get
Demands a will of steel
To be despised by all and sundry
Requires vocational zeal

His wife is really very shy
She doesn't get out often
She never has a stitch to wear
But knows he'll never soften
She tries to keep him happy
And pays a heavy price
Deep down she realizes
He isn't very nice
Something died inside her
On the day that they were wed
It never was a good idea
To marry *that tight get*

He says that when its time to die
Just sling him on a skip
Give his organs to medical science
Leave the rest out on a tip
No coffin will be needed
Or tombstone nice and smart
Just a big bin liner
To throw upon the cart
But he doesn't plan to go soon
It isn't over yet
He's got to bleed the NHS
'cos he is *one tight get*

So much for the tight get
There's nothing more to add
Just don't expect much sympathy

For that unpleasant lad
But when his time is past and gone
He shifts his mortal coil
Some say his reputation
Must never, ever, spoil
Erect, perhaps, a statue
Of marble, in concrete set
With a most sincere carving
'Sod off! You *one tight get!*'

Raftery's Flip-Flop Solution

It is very often stated that these are dreadful times
With violence in the home and in the street
Shaven-headed psychos committing lots of crimes
Unpleasant people whom you wouldn't care to meet
Now many feel despondent and foresee no improvement
It's an ongoing, problematic situation
Yet I would assert that this is too defeatist
Some very simple steps could soon be taken
To clean up the streets and the city's trouble spots
Eradicating sociopathic hoodlums
So allow me to expound my unparalleled wisdom
It's called *Raftery's flip-flop solution*

When these citizens are intent on anti social behaviour
Being nauseating and depraved in public places
Swilling cans of lager and dropping down their trousers
Screaming obscenities from smirking faces
Forcibly at gunpoint remove their chosen footwear
No discussion needed, it's a very simple rule
Then take a box of matches, put the trainers on the ground
And soak them completely in high-octane lighter fuel
They probably will protest when they see what happens next
As an inevitable conflagration then ensues
No doubt they they'll moan a bit and maybe use some rude words
Like 'What the *flip* are we supposed to do for shoes?'
Then into the back of the van the officer slowly reaches
While the wayward youth wails and whines and hops
Then stares in disbelief at his substituted footwear
A brand new pair of mass-produced flip-flops

You cannot be a menace to society in flip-flops
You cannot rob old ladies and steal their pension books

You can't go on the rampage in your garish football gear
People would just laugh at you and give you funny looks
You cannot be a hooligan when you're wearing flip-flops
Somehow it just would not seem right
You cannot run at speed to get the other team's supporters
You wouldn't have the stomach for a fight
You cannot go shoplifting or picking people's pockets
All this sort of thing then quickly stops
People would say, 'Keep your eye upon that fella,
He's usually up to no good in them flip-flops'

Now some people may believe that this plan will never work
And that from the very outset it is cursed
But at least it's cost effective and will boost the flip-flop market
So please remember where you heard it first

Soldiering Boy

Ecstatic yells as the big ship set sail
Way back in the year 82
Ruling Britannia sent you on your way
Engulfed in the red, white and blue
Setting off on a great, bold adventure
An outdated colonial war
A man has to do what he joined up to do
What else do we have soldiers for?

But what will you do then ex-soldiering boy
When the army is all done with you?
Where will you run to ex-soldiering boy
When your soldiering days are all through?

The screaming and yelling cut into your brain
As scorched skin was sliced from the bone
Unlike the scenes in old Hollywood films
Where reality must never be shown
Death comes in so many disguises
And sometimes its not cut and dried
And sometimes the ones who are living
Would change places with those who had died

One hundred thousand - the payment was fixed
The price of the leg left behind
And now you must learn to walk on a crutch
And line up with the crippled and blind
Kept out of sight at the victory parade
It doesn't look good on the screen
Finding new friends that you don't really need
With improbable quick money schemes

And now that the bad business deals fallen through
And new friends are slipping away

These are the true fortunes of war
The harrowing price that you pay
Gone are your dreams and ambitions
To the sound of the piper's sad tune
And all hopes of a better tomorrow
Must fade like your youth -all too soon

So what will you do now ex-soldiering boy
Now the army is all done with you?
Nowhere to run to ex-soldiering boy
Now your soldiering days are all through

It Came in The Night

It came in the night and parked itself near Uncle Bernard's allotment shed
When Bernard came for his secateurs he took one look and fled
He ran till his wellies felt like glue and he could go no further
Then fell down on the pavement and screamed and bawled blue murder
Outside the hardware store he lay with just one thing in mind
Fearing he'd been followed and it might creep up from behind
Mrs Bickerdike dropped her shopping bag and gaped at him in fright
But the only words that he could say were *it came in the night*

A man came from the Civic Hall and said that it was toxic refuse
Adding that it would cost Bernard a bob or two in order to get it moved
The Inland Revenue said that a benefactor must have left it behind
And that Bernard would have more tax to pay on a benefit in kind
The local UFO organisation said it was an alien life force
The new age doctor laid his hands on it and said it was a vital life source
Then crowds all came in search of a cure, or just to catch a sight
Then rang relations on mobile phones saying *it came in the night*

The Daily Mail gravely dismissed it as cynical political spin
The Daily Express was quite outraged and said no more should be let in
A man emerged out from the Tower far away in London town
Pompously pronouncing that it was now the property of the crown
He said 'you are deeply honoured – it will be treasured by Prince William'
Bernard said, 'It belongs to me but - you can have it for 23 million!
If you won't cough up, that's just too bad, you can go and fly a kite
It's not mentioned in any statute book, *it came in the night'*

Look North did an interview and Bernard became a local hero
He even ended up getting his very own late night raunchy chat show
He now has a column in the local paper where he calls a spade a spade
He is keen to make some easy cash before his new fame starts to fade
Spielberg came and made a film starring Tom Cruise in the lead role
And Jennifer Lopez took her clothes off and caught her death of cold
The allotment is now a tourist haunt maintained by Mrs Bickerdike
Who enchants pilgrims with her surreal saga - *'it came in the night'*

One more thing …………..

To check out the further adventures of Raftery the Poet visit his exciting website at

www.qi5.co.uk/rafterythepoet

Further copies of Raftery's poetry collection

Smart Boy Wanted

may be obtained by contacting

**Smithy Publications
PO Box 32
Leeds
LS8 2BS**